Today is a Great Day to Show Your Shine

~ Judy Kay Mausolf

This book is dedicated to:

My favorite person in this world, my husband, Steve Mausolf, the one I laugh with, grow with, dream with, and love. Thank you for believing I can do anything.

To my six brothers and sisters, Lorraine, Leatrice, David, Jeanette, Ken, and Jim—they keep me grounded and real. I listed their names in order from oldest to youngest to avoid getting any grief over favoritism later.

To my parents, Ione and Clem Miller, who taught me faith, hope, and common sense, and gave me the backbone to persevere. Thank you, Mom and Dad. I love you and miss you daily.

TABLE OF CONTENTS

An Evolutionary Journey to Get Out of
Your Way and On Your Way to Success!

RISE &
SHINE!

Cover and Interior Design by Jaad

ISBN 13: 978-0-9825912-6-0

Library of Congress Catalog Number: 2010942511

Printed in the United States of America

First Printing: January 2011

23 22 21 20   8 7 6 5

Judy Kay Mausolf
18051 Jay Court
Lakeville, MN 55044
612-701-4922
www.PracticeSolutionsInc.net

"There are people who put their dreams in a little box and say, 'Yes, of course, I've got dreams.' Then they put the box away and bring it out once in awhile to look in it, and yep, they're still in there. It takes an uncommon amount of guts to put your dreams on the line, to hold them up to the world."

~ Erma Bombeck

FOREWORD

The why's in life always precede the how's!

Why do some people succeed from very difficult backgrounds when others from wonderful backgrounds fail?

Why do some people start each day with unmitigated joy, midst myriad circumstances, when others find a happy start to a day almost an impossibility?

Why do some people see others in their lives as those to serve while others see themselves as deserving of being served only?

We could go on and on, but you get the gist.

It is a decision—a personal, daily, decision for happiness, for contentment, for abundance versus scarcity for seeing the cup half full or literally full to overflowing.

"Today is a Great Day to Show Your Shine" is the byline which our author signs her correspondence. It is the core of her belief system, the compass of her life, and her mantra for serving others in this day, not waiting until the opportunity which may never come again.

Judy Kay Mausolf did not start with a silver spoon in her mouth, but with a "silver space in her heart" for being and becoming all she was meant by her Creator to be. What is a silver space in her heart?

It is that sterling determination to overcome the obstacles that life certainly will place in our path. It is the attitude of privilege and promise toward self and others, rather than defeat and discouragement.

It is the belief that we all have potential for gladness in what we do, what we are, and how we share our giftedness with others.

As is soon realized, this is an evolving journey of expectation, growth, and joy! The journey is the destination; it is the defining path that we take versus the path of discouragement and defeat.

Welcome to the journey.

I encourage you to live it for yourself. This is a working manual that inspires but also practically spells out the steps that truly successful people take to find amazing significance in life.

I join you in finding joy in the journey!

Naomi Rhode, CSP, CPAE Speaker Hall of Fame
Past President National Speakers Association
Past President Global Speakers Association
Speaker, Author, Speaking/Life Coach
Co-Founder SmartPractice

Sunrise in Sausalito, California

We Choose Our Life!

Why am I writing this book—hmmm.

I tell others, "This is By the Book of Judy," when I share my worldly advice. Therefore, I feel it is necessary to write at least one book during my lifetime.

Dad always said I was going to run out of words by the time I was five. Not a betting woman, I decided to put my beliefs in writing—just in case I really do run out.

I am a performance coach. I coach others on how to succeed at being happy, healthy, and high performing. Life isn't meant to be hard. Life is a gift. We choose how we live it. Some of us get that. Some of us don't. This book is to help create awareness how we can choose our lives and make them awesome. This book is an evolutionary journey for succeeding in living a life you choose and love.

Overcome Limiting Beliefs to Rewrite Your Story

We'll start the evolutionary journey where it all begins, with beliefs.

Most of our beliefs can be traced back to our early lives. I'm the youngest of seven and am blessed with a great family. I grew up on a farm in North Dakota and the closest town, St. Anthony, was four miles away. The town offered a small mom-and-pop grocery store, a school, a church, and a bar. The population boasted twenty-one residents, maybe, on a good day. We didn't have a lot of money so Mom would cut our hair to help make ends meet. I wasn't the prettiest girl in school. I had what we called a "pixie" back then. It was a short bob cut. Mom would start out by placing Scotch Tape on my bangs. She would hold my bangs down and cut above the tape. When she let them go, they would stand straight up.

My bangs were always very short and very crooked. I had a big wide space between my front teeth and tons of freckles. Do you get the visual? Not your typical beauty queen.

My siblings and me; I am the happy one in the tie.

I loved watching beauty pageants. I'm watching *Miss America* with my mom. And I am so excited. First of all, you may not realize how lucky I was to be able to watch the pageant. It was 1965 and back then we only had one TV, a big old brown Philco, which meant everybody had to watch the same show.

So, I am sitting next to my mom saying, "Mom, Mom, Mom, do you think I could be Miss America someday? Huh, Mom?" She just smiled and looked at me with the crooked haircut, tooth space, and freckles. "Oh, Honey, you're a little ray of sunshine. If you believe in yourself and you show that shine to the world, I think you can be whatever you want to be." In that one powerful statement she helped a five-year-old little girl start to believe in herself.

I would like you to think back to your childhood. Was there someone who helped you to believe in yourself? Maybe it was a parent, teacher, brother, or sister, someone who told you that

Mom and Dad in their early years

you had potential. Do you remember how what they said made you feel?

~~~~~~

"See, we don't become what we want in life; we become what we believe."

~ Judy Kay Mausolf

~~~~~~

What we believe determines our actions and our actions generate our outcome. It is not important whether the little girl (me) becomes Miss America or not. By the way, my interests led me elsewhere, but what is important is the fact that I learned to believe in myself. Whatever it is we desire in life—happiness, respect, more money, less stress—our success always depends on our beliefs.

"Internal messages always generate the external."

~ Judy Kay Mausolf

I have met so many amazing and wonderful people who can't, don't, or won't see their own potential lives. Their limiting beliefs are stopping them from taking even the first steps to succeed and are sabotaging them from reaching their dreams. We can either empower or *un-power* ourselves, depending on the stories we repeatedly play over and over in our minds. Those stories start at a very early age. Think about the stories that stop you from going after what you want in life and being the person you want to be. Aren't you tired of those stories by now?

Challenge those not-enough thoughts (NETs)—not rich enough, pretty enough, smart enough. Enough with the enough's. The next time you are asked to do something that you would like to do, say, "I can," even if you don't know all the answers or how to's. Whenever we tell ourselves we can do something, we empower ourselves to take the first step to succeed. Our mind believes what it thinks. Continue to challenge and overcome those NETs taking up space in your head.

"We are all responsible for ourselves; you create your own reality by the way you think and therefore act."

~ Oprah Winfrey

Action Plan

* Identify your limiting beliefs—Make a list of all the reasons you think you can't or shouldn't do something. Then go back and challenge each one by saying, "If this were really true, what's something else I could do to accomplish it?"

* Set new goals and objectives—Make a list of all your dreams and desires and prioritize the list.

* Create a step-by-step process—Start with your number one priority and write down each step you will take to accomplish your goal. Answer what, when, where, why, and how to create your steps. For example, will you need more training, education, or experience and, if so, when, where, why, and how?

* Establish timelines—Write down by what date you will accomplish each step; be specific—example: by the first quarter or a certain month. Being specific allows you to

hold yourself accountable, whereas saying you want to accomplish something in a year has a tendency to give you permission to leave things to the end of the year. Accountability happens when you set timelines for each step.

* Practice, practice, and practice verbal skills, role playing, the entire walk-through before you take your new ideas to your family, friends, colleagues, and potential clients. Practicing is what will empower you to feel confident to implement your new ideas.

* Take the first step even though you may not know all the answers. You don't have to know all the nuances of every step, just what to do to take the very first step. In this day of information and technology, you'll discover whatever you need to know as you need it. As you take each step towards your goals and dreams, you increase awareness of what else you need to progress, and you'll find what you need when you need it.

Discover Your Journey, Define Direction, and Clarify Vision

"The best way to predict the future is create it."

~ Peter Drucker

If you want to create your future, you need to know who you are at your core and the direction you want to head. What do you want to do in your life besides just get up, go to work, come home, and go to bed? Maybe for some of us that is enough, but for most of us, we want more out of life.

One of the first questions I ask when I am coaching is, "What is your vision for your life?" Usually, I hear, "Hmmm, I'm not really sure. I haven't really taken the time to sit down and think it through."

Think about the journey you are currently on. Does it reflect your core beliefs and your vision for the future, or are you just responding to what life brings your way?

Rewind back to January of 2008. I decided to put together a vision board to help clarify my goals and objectives. I cut out pictures, words, and quotes to signify all my personal and professional goals and hung it on the wall in my office across from my desk. Every time I look up I can see it.

Forward to February first. I receive an email from the *Oprah Winfrey Show*. This is not unusual because I had signed up to receive information on the topics for the week and if there were any last-minute tickets available for the show. I have wanted to go to the *Oprah Show* for at least ten years and have tried continually without success. I am swamped with work and don't have time to watch any shows, and there are never any last-minute tickets available.

I decide to delete the email without opening it. As I am about to hit the delete button, I look up and smack dab in the middle of my vision board is a picture of Oprah and above it reads, "Go to the *Oprah Show.*" It was one of my goals and objectives, so I feel the least I can do is click on the link to prove there aren't any last-minute tickets.

I click on the link and there *are* last-minute tickets, and all I need to do is respond in two thousand words or fewer why I would be a good match for the audience. Get this, the show's topic is vision boards. It's a sign.

I respond why I am a good match and sign off with, "See you next Tuesday," the day of the show. I hit send with one hand and pick up the phone with the other to call my cousin Holly.

We have an agreement that whoever wins tickets to the *Oprah Show,* the other will be her guest. "Holly, its Jude, pack your bags and get a sitter, we're going to *Oprah* next Tuesday." I tell her the story of the vision board; we both laugh and hang up. That was Thursday evening.

Friday morning I get a call from Sherry at the *Oprah Winfrey Show*. "Judy, would you like to attend the *Oprah Winfrey Show* and bring three of your friends as guests next Tuesday, February 6, 2008?" "You bet."

Holly, Perri, Sheri, and I went and we had an amazing time. Was it magic? Was it coincidence? If you recall, I was about ready to hit delete on that email. When I looked up and saw, "Go to the *Oprah Show*," it brought that goal and objective to the top of my mind. When we are clear on our goals and objectives, we become clear on the actions to take to make them reality.

Vision boards aren't magical or secret and don't work if they are in a closet somewhere. In fact, the name "vision" is a great

My Vision Board

name for them because they need to be in sight to work to keep your goals and objectives in your sight and at the top of your mind.

You can use other methods instead such as lists, refrigerator reminders, or journals; my husband has his on his ever-changing screensaver.

Here is how you can apply this to your life.

Action Plan

* List your personal and professional goals for this year. Regardless of the date, start your year right now. Create a vision year versus a calendar year. If you already have a long-term vision, review, evaluate, and update your vision when necessary. Ask yourself, "Does my vision still reflect my beliefs and vision for the future?" We continue to grow

and change every day; therefore, our vision may grow and change as well.

* Clarify goals and objectives for the year—think about what you want to accomplish this year. Write all your ideas down, and then prioritize the list.

* Define who can help you achieve what you want to achieve. What relationships do you need to develop?

* What are the steps you need to take to accomplish your goals and objectives—for example, will you need more training, education, or experience, and if so, when, where, why, and how?

* Decide when you will accomplish each step. Write down by what date you will accomplish each step. As I mentioned in the first chapter on beliefs, be specific (example: by the first quarter or by a certain month). Being specific will allow you to hold yourself accountable.

* Monitor your progress monthly. Once a month, review your progress. Are you where you need to be to succeed at reaching your goals in the timeline you established? If not, focus on completing the steps necessary to get you back on track. If you are ahead, good for you; keep going. It is always better to have a little cushion for the hiccups in life.

"Focus your energy on each day. Don't let the confusion of the past or the fear of the future cloud your vision."

~ Vicky Mitchener

Rainbows on the Journey

Attain an Awesome Attitude and Mindset

Flower Market

You may have heard our attitude determines our altitude in life. Our attitude affects our altitude by creating positive or negative energy in the environment around us. The energy we create generates either our success or our failure based on the Law of Resonance.

The Law of Resonance is "like seeks like," based on the frequency of energy emitted from each source.

All energy has different vibrational frequencies. Positive energy seeks other positive energy with the same frequency, and negative energy seeks other negative energy with the same frequency.

Think about a day when your world seemed friendlier. The birds sang louder, the sun shined brighter, and people even let you merge into traffic. We have all had one of those days where we think, "Wow, if every day could be like today, it would be awesome." Maybe they can be. I wonder what your role was in

"Rain and sun are to the flower as praise and encouragement are to the human spirit."

~ Mario Fernandez

that day that was so awesome. I wonder what mood you were in when it started. I wonder what you wearing, how it made you feel, and if you were smiling.

When we feel good about ourselves, we radiate positive energy. The energy we put out there always resonates back to us. We do create our environment whether it is positive or negative.

In October of 2006, my husband, Steve, and I went on this fabulous trip to Como, Italy. It's this beautiful, old, Italian village nestled at the base of the Alps on Lake Como right between Milan and Switzerland. Steve and I love to walk and on the first morning's walk we see the locals heading to work. They are smiling, waving, and greeting each other with a "*Buongiorno.*" I think, *How cool; I am going to do that!* So, I start smiling, waving, and greeting with a "*Buongiorno.*"

Well, unbeknownst to me, the Italians in Como, Italy, think it is superficial to smile and greet people they don't know, so they don't. I am *buongiorning* away and getting no responses.

By the second day, Steve says, "Jude, give it up; they're not going to smile at you."

Well, to me that's like holding a red flag in front of a bull. It became my goal to get at least one person to smile at me. First of all, because I believe in the Law of Resonance, but, more importantly, I just wanted to prove Steve wrong. I continue to smile and *buongiorno* away and still no response.

On day five, I see this little old woman walking towards us and about one hundred feet apart we make eye contact. I am

Zoe, Yorkie with an Awesome Attitude

beaming at her, high-beam; she is scowling at me. I continue to beam; she continues to scowl. We get closer; I am still smiling, but she is no longer scowling. I see the right side of her lip start to twitch, and as we pass, she looks up at me and smiles for a second and quickly looks down. I look back at her; she is looking back at me. She smiles again, shakes her head as if to say silly American, and continues on her way. A smile works even in Como, Italy, to create positive energy in our environment.

Not only does attitude affect our environment, it also affects our health. Bad attitudes are harmful to our health. Consistent negative thoughts, words, or actions (such as anger, gossip, or complaining), whether we are the giver, or the receiver, or even just in the vicinity, change the electricity in our brains, which changes the energy in our bodies. The organs that need that energy are no longer nourished and they get disease and sometimes they die. Attitude is everything in creating a happy, healthy environment. Here is how you can create an awesome attitude.

Check Buddy

Action Plan

☼ Check Buddy

* Have a meeting with those you surround yourself with. Discuss as a group the attitude you want in your environment and the actions and behaviors necessary to create this type of attitude. Ask someone to be your check buddy. A check buddy is first person you see in the day to check in with and hold each other accountable to a level of attitude. Throughout the rest of day, any one of the check buddies can hold another check buddy accountable to the actions and behaviors that the family or co-workers established. It is important to agree on a word you can say to each other in a sincere and caring manner to get each other's attention to help get a positive attitude back. It could be a word as simple as smile.

Smile & Shine Band

☼ Smile & Shine Band

❋ Find something to create awareness to remember to smile for yourself and others. I promote the use of my orange rubber bracelet inscribed with the words, "Smile & Shine." Smile energy is extremely powerful and wide spreading. A smile instantly creates positive energy in the environment and uplifts the mindsets of the giver, the receiver, and everyone in the vicinity.

☼ Ray for the Day

❋ Start your day out with a positive quote for the day, what I refer to as a "Ray for the Day." You can find uplifting quotes by Googling uplifting quotes. Reading a positive quote at the start of the day helps kick off the day with positive energy.

Sunrise in Cancun, Mexico

☼ Kudos Environment

* What I mean by a kudos environment is creating a culture of acknowledgment. To create a kudos environment, it is important to know and be aware of what is good and right in your environment. Most people see what's negative and wrong in their environment. Instead, focus on what is good and right and verbally reward each other with statements such as, "I am proud of you," "Great job," "Way to go," "Thank you," or just "Kudos." In a very short time everyone will begin to feel recognized, important, and cared about because they know they are being seen and praised on a daily basis. I love this kudos stuff because it really works. It only takes one person to get the ball rolling in the right direction. The person could be you. You don't need permission to start. You just start by acknowledging and rewarding what is good and right—good moods, good attitude, uplifting mindsets, even just a smile.

"Every day is my best day; this is my life. I'm not going to have this moment again."

~ Bernie Siegel

Communicate, Connect, and Relate Successfully to Others

Hot Air Balloon Ride in Napa, California

Our success depends greatly on how well we communicate in our personal and professional lives. When we communicate openly, positively, and effectively, we inspire connections and build sincere, strong, sustaining relationships. Our ceiling of success then becomes like the old expression, *The sky's the limit*.

"The problem with communication is the illusion it has been accomplished."

~ George Bernard Shaw

Communication Breakdowns

It is important to know the breakdowns that get in the way of communication in order to avoid them. Personal truths is the number one breakdown in communication. When we interact with others, we are always coming from a place filled with our own experiences. Our expectations differ because of our unique and individual beliefs, opinions, and assumptions based on our experiences. These expectations become our personal truths upon which we base judgments of right and wrong. To help you remember the concept, see the first letters of each word; it spells out the word *B.O.A.T.* **B**eliefs, **O**pinions, **A**ssumptions, therefore, are **T**ruths based on our experiences.

We all have unique and individual experiences, yet we expect each other to think, act, and respond the same. These are some false expectations that can get us into trouble. Others must behave in the same manner as we do or their behavior is wrong. Another person's behavior must mean the same as ours if we did that same behavior. We get in a disagreement because others disagree with our opinions. These are examples of expectations based on personal truths. Once we understand that our personal

B.O.A.T. - Marina in Sausalito, California

17-Mile Drive, Monterey, California

truths (how we judge the world by what is right and wrong) are based on the unique and individual experiences we have, we can no longer believe that our answer is the only right answer.

The *Poison Triangle of Mistrust* is another breakdown that is lethal to communication.

This happens when one person has an issue with a second person and takes that issue to a third person. In many cases it's because we don't want to hurt that first person's feelings, and we don't realize the full implications of our action. Many of us may refer to this as gossip or talking behind one's back.

It is important to understand that if you are on the receiving end of gossip, you are just as responsible as if you are the initiator. You play a fifty-fifty role. If the gossiper has no one to tell, the gossip stops. To prevent gossip, avoid talking to a third person regarding the question, concern, or conflict unless the third person is responsible for conflict resolution. If you take it to another person, you will create the *Poison Triangle of Mistrust*. If you turned the tables around and someone was talking about you, you would no longer trust that person or even want to talk to him or her.

Action Plan

☼ Understand and Respect Personal Truths

* Listen to their truths.

* Share your truths.

* It's never about who is right or wrong.

* Agree on a third answer that works for both of the truths.

* It is important that we as individuals make a personal commitment to be *open, respectful, and understanding* of each other's personal truths; it is what will enable us to communicate and interact effectively with others.

✻ Avoid Poison Triangle of Mistrust

* Talk directly to the person with whom you have a question, concern, or conflict.

* Ask to set up time to meet.

* Avoid talking to anyone else about the issue.

* Avoid having a negative attitude.

* Use the phrase, "This didn't work"—don't personalize.

* Listen calmly.

* Share both sides.

* Discuss and come to a solution.

* Hold each other accountable.

* If not resolved, all parties involved get together with whomever is responsible for conflict resolution.

~~~~~~

"Once a human being has arrived on this earth, communication is the largest single factor determining what kinds of relationships he makes with others and what happens to him."
~ Virginia Satir

~~~~~~

Radiate a Congruent Appearance with Your Core Beliefs and Goals

What does your appearance resonate?

Think about the first impression you make when you meet someone. Because the first impression happens in the first fifteen seconds, we are judged based solely on our appearance. What do others see and assume about you? Is it positive and congruent with you at your core? Take a long look at yourself in the mirror. Is their perception of you what you mean to resonate? We have one chance to make a first impression. Therefore, it is imperative that our appearance be positive and congruent with our core beliefs and vision for the future.

It is human nature to look for things to reinforce what we already believe. If we have a negative first impression of someone, we will look for more negative things to reinforce our beliefs. Even if it means stretching parameters to include what would normally be considered neutral, what was acceptable now becomes negative.

It works the same way with positive looking for positive. That is why it is so important to make a positive first impression. It is also important that our appearance be congruent with who we are, where we want to go in life, and how we want to be perceived. Otherwise, we send a mixed signal and create doubt, confusion, and mistrust in others when they have to decide what is really true about us. Hair, makeup, nails, body adornments, and the styles and colors of clothes we wear all help create a congruent, positive first impression.

Action Plan

There are three questions to ask yourself to help you radiate a successful appearance that's congruent with your core beliefs and goals.

1. Does it look good on me?

2. Do I love it?

3. Is it congruent with my core beliefs, vision for the future, and the image I want to radiate?

Number three is the most important of all when deciding a successful look. It may look good, you may love it, but it may not be congruent with your core beliefs, vision for the future, or image you want to radiate. If it isn't congruent with all three, don't buy it or wear it. Make that first impression that truly reflects you.

"Years may wrinkle the skin, but to give up enthusiasm wrinkles the soul."

~ Samuel Ullman

Judy and Steve, Happy Souls!

Master Accountability; Assume Responsibility for Your Life

J ust hearing the word accountability can give the majority of us an *ugh* feeling. What usually pops into our minds are the why-we-can't-do-it thoughts. "How can I fit this into my already busy schedule?" "What if don't know how to do it?" Or the most restricting of question of all, "What if I fail?" If you look up the meaning of accountability in the dictionary, it's no wonder many of us have such a visceral response to the word. Here are just a few definitions: affliction, blame, burden, concern, difficulty, excess baggage, fault, guilt, hardship, liability, load, punishment, strain, trouble, work-worry. Whew! I am definitely getting the picture accountability is not something most of us want to be a part of.

What if we shoved all those descriptions aside and merely looked at accountability as being the ability to count on someone else to do something? Would that really be so bad?

If we could count on someone else we could:

* Free our thoughts and actions to focus on something new.

* Utilize the strengths of others greater than our own.

* Build stronger relationships by being able to rely on each other.

Accountability in this light is really a win-win for the giver and the receiver.

Every Sunday morning, I can count on my husband, Steve, to magically prepare the most delicious fried eggs, flattened to my desired perfection (squished three times with the spatula), and blanketed in fresh goat cheese, basil, and other herbs. In this case, Steve is the giver of accountability and I am the receiver of accountability. Every Sunday morning, Steve can count on me to have filled the fridge with fresh eggs, cheese, and herbs in

Steve (husband) and Me in Sausalito, California

order for him to create his magic. Steve is now the receiver of accountability and I am the giver of accountability. The lines easily get blurred between who is the giver and who is the receiver of accountability and who wins the most.

Steve's Sunday Fried Eggs

Magic

"The magic in mastering accountability is everyone wins!"

– Judy Kay Mausolf

Action Plan

* Start with **Me** because that's where accountability begins. When we commit to taking personal responsibility for a task or a behavior and follow up with actions that support our commitment, we create accountability.

* The **Baby** is task management, which is often difficult to achieve. There is not a standard protocol for task management. Therefore, we have many different expectations, resulting in many different actions, resulting in many different outcomes, ending in a lack of accountability. Task management is what we will refer to as "the Baby."

* The tasks you are responsible to complete on a daily basis are your babies. You are the parent responsible for the care of the babies. If you cannot take care of your baby, you need to find someone to take over the care of your baby for the day. We call this person the babysitter. Parents may only request a babysitter for their babies (tasks) that must be completed during the current day.

* The parent cannot just leave the baby on the counter or the floor in a baby pile or propped up somewhere in a corner hoping someone will see it and take care for it. The parent can-

not toss the baby at another person walking by and hope that person catches the baby. They cannot force the care of their baby on another person. *These are some things that happen with our tasks when we feel we are too busy.*

* Parents must ask another person to take over the care of their baby. The babysitter must agree before the parent can hand over the care of the baby.

* The parent's role is not complete until the babysitter is informed exactly about what the parent has done so far to care for the baby and the expectations to complete the care of the baby for the day.

* The babysitter is now responsible to update the parent at the end of the day regarding the care completed. If, for some reason, the babysitter gets too busy to care for the baby, the babysitter cannot just give the baby back to the parent and say, "I can't do it." The babysitter has assumed responsibil-

Rylee, the Baby

ity for the baby's care. The babysitter can ask the parents if they can take the baby back. However, if the parent can't, the babysitter is responsible to find another babysitter who will agree to take over the care of the baby (by following the same protocol). The initial babysitter must inform the parent who will be taking over the care of the baby.

* At the end of the day, the current babysitter is now responsible to hand the baby back to the parent and update the parent regarding the care completed.

* Treating a task like a baby will create a high standard of accountability for managing tasks.

* The **Elephant** is behavior management and the third component to mastering accountability.

  ○ Establish a standard of behavior congruent with your beliefs, vision for the future, and image you want to

The Elephant

radiate, to include attitude, communication, and actions.

- ☼ Hold yourself accountable, no exclusions or exceptions.

- ☼ Monitor your behavior daily by reviewing the previous day's successes and growth opportunities.

- ☼ Maintain that standard of behavior. This means no individual opt outs depending on the day or how you feel. If maintaining a certain behavior isn't working for you, re-evaluate it and revise it to fit your goals.

The next time you are asked to take on something new, to be accountable, respond with gusto, "You can count on me." Even if you don't know all the answers, just dive in and see who really wins in the end.

"Everything in your life has led you to here. Now, what are you going to do with it?"

~ Margaret Prusan

Live Authentically;
Be Faithful to Internal,
Not External, Ideas

Authenticity is the degree to which one is true to one's own personality, spirit, or character, despite the pressures of the world.

It's us being real to who we are at our core. The real deal! I often think of how simple relationships, and the world in general, would be if things were as they seemed to be.

With all the noise going on around us, we can easily lose who we are and what is important to us. The noise I am talking about is all the questions and suggestions we hear from well-intending others. These seemingly innocent questions and suggestions block the path to living authentically—statements like, "You should have," "You must do," and "Why aren't you," just to name a few. We have all heard at least one of these, if not all of the following: "You must do this to succeed in business," or

100%
the real deal

"Isn't it time you get married (or have kids or get a real job or get a life or...)."

Stop the noise for a moment, for a second, maybe a little longer. For some of us, we may need a few days, weeks, months, or even years. There are no rights or wrongs or rules or regulations in finding your authentic self. It's whatever time it takes you to breathe, dig deep inside, and find what really matters to you at your core.

Action Plan

* It is important to know who we are at our core. When we began to make decisions and live a life based on what has meaning to us and not others, we become our genuine authentic self. You will know when you are living your authentic self. Tremendous feelings of freedom to be who you are, along with gratitude and celebration for life, will embrace you.

* Find out what is important and real to you. What empowers, energizes, and exhilarates you to live life to the fullest? Listen to what your core (gut) is telling you. Here's essence of how we know it is our core versus our intellect talking to us: our intellect will try to explain and reason things out in long sentences, for some of us in paragraphs or even a short book. Don't laugh; you know who you are. Whereas, our core response is concise and clear and leaves us no room for doubt. Yes, no, stay, go, don't do it, do it, are examples of what comes from our core.

* The more closely we listen and tune into our core, the easier it becomes to hear. Eventually it becomes so loud we can't miss it even if we want to. Sometimes our core message challenges us to tread in new waters and sometimes it's intimidating. Trust your core; it is never wrong. It is an expert in the essence of you.

* Once you know your authentic self, it's time to show it. Initially, showing our authentic self can be intimidating. Thoughts like, *what if they don't like me, what if they laugh and make fun of me, or what if they don't accept me* can haunt us. In reality, people are drawn to people who are the real deal. Our sense of people's authenticity has an enormous impact on how much we trust them, how comfortable we are with them, and how willing we are to follow them. Showing your authentic self is a vital, essential piece that builds trust and respect. If people detect that you are not who you say you are, they lose trust and respect for you. Be genuine, don't manipulate. Be true to yourself and your beliefs. When we show who we really are and what we are passionate about, our message comes across loud and clear and rings true.

It's time you let people know you, the real deal, your authentic self. Tune in and see what manifests in your life.

"The authentic self is the soul made visible."

~ Sarah Ban

CHAPTER EIGHT

Be Consistent With Your Value System and Exemplify Integrity

Integrity means sticking firmly to a moral code, reflected in honesty and harmony in what one thinks, says, and does. Integrity means doing the right thing, even if nobody is watching.

"Integrity is what we do, what we say, and what we say we do."

- Don Galer

My parents raised me to believe that a person's word and name were golden. No matter what events happened in life, I could overcome all things if I always kept my word. Keeping my word meant I had integrity. A person was considered rich if he or she had integrity. Family, friends, and colleagues would gladly lend whatever was needed. Their willingness to give was based

Tree in Napa Valley, California

on trust, respect, reliability, and honesty, the main characteristics of one who has integrity.

Action Plan

* Tell the truth, even in the small things.

* Enlist the help of others if you face difficult decisions.

* Acknowledge mistakes, apologize, and make amends.

* Develop a work and home environment that supports the personal integrity of others.

* Be true to yourself and follow your own path.

* Keep your word.

* Have a cause or a purpose not just about you.

* Let your actions speak louder than words.

* Lead by example.

* Promote those who show an ability to be trusted.

* Have ethical consistency and predictability.

~~~~~~

"Success is the ability to lay your head on your pillow at night with your integrity uncompromised."

~ Tanja Diamond

~~~~~~

Gus! Integrity Uncompromised

Appreciate, Be Thankful, and Embrace Gratitude for What Is

Gratitude is the quality or feeling of being grateful or thankful for what is in your life at the moment. Many of us get so busy in our lives we no longer see what we have as gifts; instead, we take them for granted. It is not until we lose our gifts that we remember how much they mean to us. Life becomes routine and things become just normal, and we falsely believe normal will last forever.

Difficult times can force us to realize there are no guarantees in life and things are really only as they are for the moment. When we realize things in life, and life itself, are temporary, we are inclined to no longer take them for granted. We become grateful for what is.

When we push aside the noise, it becomes easy to be embraced with gratitude for all our blessings. How clear it all becomes—colors are more vibrant, sounds are musical, smells are sweeter, relationships have become precious, and everything comes

Colors are more vibrant.

"Gratitude turns what we have into enough, and more. It turns problems into gifts, failures into success, the unexpected into perfect timing, and mistakes into important events. Gratitude makes sense of our past, brings peace for today, and creates a vision for tomorrow."

~ Melodie Beattie

alive. Or, is it really all just the same as it was before, only now we see it? The simple truth is we will never be happy with ourselves and our lives until we are grateful for what we already have. This concept may sound so simple and yet it can be so hard to master. Think about it for a moment. It is only when we give thanks and appreciate the things that already exist in our lives, when we stop comparing ourselves to others, that we find peace and happiness.

~~~~~~

"Gratefulness is the key to a happy life that we hold in our hands. If we are not grateful, then no matter how much we have we will always want to have something else or something more."

~ *David Steindl-Rast*

~~~~~~

Action Plan

* Start your day with words of gratitude. It might be as simple as, "I am grateful to be alive another day to celebrate what life has in store for me." Do you remember the old saying to count your blessings? When we get in the habit of counting our blessings, we embrace gratitude.

* Think about all the things you are grateful for such as family, friends, health, home, work, the sunshine, or even raindrops.

* In a notebook or your computer, write down the top ten things that make you feel grateful. Once you start, you'll begin to realize how many things you have to be truly grateful for.

* Appreciate the people you know and show them you appreciate them with your words and actions, appreciate things

Vineyard in Yountville, California

you have by being positive in your words and actions, appreciate the opportunities you have in life by embracing them with your words and actions.

Stop the noise and take a moment each day to look and see—really see—all the temporary gifts you have received, including life, and be grateful.

CHAPTER TEN

Enjoy, Celebrate, and Be Mindful in the Moment

In order to feel joy, we must first learn to be present and celebrate who we are and where we are right now at this moment.

Don't wait to enjoy and celebrate in life only once you reach that one special moment. Celebrate each moment of each day you live!

Watch little children playing together and you can see pure joy. Little children are in the moment and focus only on what is happening right at that moment. They aren't distracted with what happened in the past or what might happen next. All five of their senses—see, hear, touch, smell, and taste—are focused on what is happening in the present moment. When we grow older, we tend to lose focus on the moment and lose joy for the moment.

As adults, it is easy to lose our focus with all the noise and dis-tractions in our lives. We no longer focus on what is happen-

Mom and dad celebrating the moment on their 50th wedding anniversary.

ing in the present moment. We forget to see the beauty in a gnarly tree, hear the chirp of a chickadee, nestle a fuzzy duckling, breathe in the smell of a fragrant flower, and taste all life has to offer.

"Joyful people rejoice in their strengths, talents, and powers and do not compare themselves to anyone. Joy comes from rejoicing in all that you are, all that you have, all that you can be from knowing that you are a divine, a piece of God."

~ Dr. Wayne W. Dyer

Action Plan

* Start by tuning into the moment. Know and be aware of what is happening around you right now. Worrying or focusing on the past or the future does not change anything. Instead, it drains you of the energy you need to think, act, and be present in the moment. Focus only on being in the moment.

* Become aware of the beauty all around you and feel the healing powers of life. Fully experience flowers, sunrises and sunsets, mountains and beaches, and beautiful literature, music, and people.

* Become present in the moment. Breathe in deep and exhale, and before you breathe in again, focus on feeling your heartbeat and the pulse in your fingers and toes. Breathe in deep again. Now ask yourself, "How do I feel right now,

right this moment? What do I see, hear, touch, smell, and taste, that I am grateful I can experience?"

* Consciously decide to process your life in ways that focus on gratefulness for what you have and what is. See the abundance in your life. You can cultivate this attitude by refusing to allow yourself to think in terms of not having. Stop comparing yourself to others; instead, lovingly embrace yourself for who you are.

* Just for the fun of it, every so often, close your eyes, throw your head back, your hands up in the air, spin around, and shout for joy. Celebrate the moment.

Rise & Shine!

I think about the journey of life. How easy it is to be caught up in all the confusion and noise of should haves, would haves, and must haves. We lose ourselves and fail to remember who we are at our core, what is really important, and what is not.

We each have been given the gift to choose our own path and write our own story. Our story is not only what we control and make happen. It is also how we act versus react to difficult or unplanned events. Our success evolves when we engage and embrace the surprises, bumps, and roadblocks and persevere.

Your challenge, starting today, is to identify and change the limiting beliefs and stories that are stopping you from going after choosing a life you love. The truth is none of us are who we *were*. We are not even the same person we were yesterday. We are an accumulation of all our life experiences, and they continue to shape, change, and help us grow in every breath we take. It's up to each one of us to decide to act versus react to the events that happen in life—to choose the person we want to become. How exciting that every day we have the power and the opportunity to step towards our dreams. Our dreams can become our reality when we believe in ourselves. What steps are you willing to take right now, right this moment? You already have everything you need. Now it's your turn to *Rise & Shine!*

Internal

Messages

Always

Generate the

External

The journey

Me, living a life I love.

About the Author

J udy Kay Mausolf is the owner and president of Practice Solutions, Inc. She is a speaker, coach, and author who specializes in helping others maximize their performance to succeed at getting the results in life they desire. Her focus is communication, mindsets/attitude, and revitalization. She travels nationally, speaking at workshops, study club groups, seminars, and conventions, as well as coaching individuals and business owners to succeed. Judy Kay is also author and publisher of the monthly newsletter *Show Your Shine*.

Judy Kay happily resides in Lakeville, Minnesota, with her husband, Steve Mausolf, and their two furry, pseudo kids—Gus, a finely aged, orange, ten-pound Persian cat, and Zoe, an it's-all-about-me, five-pound Yorkshire terrier.